The Children of Sierra Leone

by Arama Christiana

pictures by
Stephen Taylor

Richard C. Owen Publishers, Inc.
Katonah, New York

We are the children of Sierra Leone.

Sierra Leone is our home and we love it.

When the sun comes up,
we go with our mothers to the farm.

We help plant cassava and yams

and care for the babies.

We climb the mango trees and pick the sweet juicy fruit to take to the city and sell.

Later we play games and tell stories of our great African warriors.

When the sun goes down
behind the mountains,
we count the stars in the sky.

Then we wave good night to the stars
and sing:

Stars shining overhead
Telling us to go to bed
Mama, good night, Ma
Papa, good night, Pa
Sister, good night, dear
Brother, good night, dear
Stars shining overhead
Good night
Good night.

**We hug and wish each other good dreams.
Then we go home to our beds.**